Musings on the Road of Life

Acknowledgements

Thanks to the editors of the following publications where several of the poems first appeared.

Pegasus:

"Unfinished Business"
"Hope Lives"
"Government Issue"
"The Gun Range"
"Dreams Abandoned"
"Life Lesson Learned Early"

Blood and Thunder:

"Doctor"
"Under Siege"
"He Was Disappearing"

Cover Art: Oil Painting by Tom Glover
Cover Design: Sarah Leis

ISBN: 9781720071648

Copyright: Tim Reardon, 2018

To Beverly

*who saw the gifts buried
beneath my dark side*

*encouraging me
to fertilize that soil*

and bring them to fruition

TABLE OF CONTENTS

Learning Laboratory 1
Life Lesson Learned Early 3
Skating on Thin Ice 5
Expectation 7
On Becoming an Altered Boy 9
One Red, One Blue 10
Dunmore Fun 11
The Fly Rod 14
Lost 15
The Invisible Goddess 16
Tied at the Hip 17
A Lesson Not Learned 18
Long Ago Memories 19
Money Doesn't Grow on Trees 20
A Letter I Never Received 22
The Journey Begins 24
Starting Anew 25
Long Journey Home 27
Alone in the World 29
Forgiveness 30
Anger Released 31
The Reluctant Learner 33
The Creature Within 34
We Are One 35
Joy Lost and Maybe Found 36
Taking Chances 37
Opening Doors 38
Late Life Love 39
Gardening 40
Healing at the Kitchen Sink 41
New Year's Stir Fry 42
The First Kiss 44

The M Word	45
Hope Lives	46
Home	47
Overs	48
Goodbye Sweetie	50
The Midnight Bandit	51
Another Bullet	53
Scarred	54
Under Siege	55
Doctor	58
He is Disappearing	59
Disappearing Friends	61
In Memory of my Friend Hyla	64
Servants	65
Lunch at Ables	66
The Silent Minority	68
For our Friend Peri Ann	69
Someone Else's Child	70
Thanksgiving at the Farm	71
Company Rules	73
On Finding Peace	74
My Own Paradise Lost	75
Don't Tread on Me	76
Is this Football or What	77
Winter Golf	79
The Pied Piper and Feral Pigs: A Fable	80
A Dreadful Morning	81
The Hidden Hero's Journey	82
The Aquarius Male	84
Spring	85
A Mother's Sadness	86
Kilnamartyra	88
Government Issue	89
The Gun Range	90

Unfinished Business 92
Dreams Abandoned 94
Wartime Romance 96
Journey Home 98

*I decided to start anew
to strip away what I
had been taught
and to trust as true
my own thinking.*

Georgia O'Keefe

Learning Laboratory

"All I really need to know
I learned in kindergarten"
Robert Fulghum

My kindergarten was Washington Street

Ma blew the whistle
come home to eat or
you will go hungry tonight

Don't throw stones at each other
which we did but stayed friends anyway
Peacemaking is worthwhile work

You can't have a BB gun
because you'll hurt someone
Which I did so I don't carry a gun

Men that shout like Mr. Linker
are dangerous so stay away from angry men
or learn how to deal with them

I learned the wrong lessons
from easy targets like Georgie Pordgie and Sissy Teddy
In time I learned we are all brothers

When the sun rose in the east
we were all the same… white Americans
when the sun settled in the west

We were… kikes, canucks, wops
lace curtain Irish and drunks
so how did we know the good guys

In time healed from darkness
today when I have memories of that neighborhood
my heart is warm as I recall the good times I had.

Life Lesson Learned Early

Easter break 1954.
Warm days and cool nights.
Adolescents yanking at the bit.
Let's go for a hike they said, it's less than a mile to the peak.
We can go up, stay a day, come back and wow the girls with
our exploits.

Knapsacks packed with cans of fruit, beans,
hot dogs and bread, ponchos for the rain,
sleeping bags and a trusty .22 rifle.
Bucklin Trailhead on the Wheelerville Road
was the jumping off point for their great adventure.
These Frodo and Sam explorers sprang forward,
unaware of the travails ahead in the green forest.

Before long the moss and fallen needles
began to turn white from a late winter storm.
They pressed on, thinking only of the mountain peak
and the cabin with its stock of firewood.
The closer they came to their destination
the deeper the snow became and the harder the crust.
Tim was beaten down. His legs ached and bled from the
    crusting snow.

I can't go any farther, he said.
Paul urged him on promising they were almost at the top.
But Tim didn't think he had anything left to give. He quit
settled into a snow cave and waited for tomorrow.
Paul went on and found their cabin only fifty yards away.
He hollered down and urged his friend to move on.

Tim dug himself out of the cave and pushed on to the top.
Finally there, he unpacked his gear and collapsed on the
    wooden bunk.

The shame of quitting began gnawing at him that day and
    lasted for decades.
Loser continually echoed around in his brain.
But, unconsciously something told him quitting was not
    an option.
Tim had many failures after that experience,
and no matter how tough the journey, he never quit.

Years later Tim forgave an inexperienced kid for that failure
    on the mountain.
And the other failures in his life.

Skating on Thin Ice

Remember when the old man said,
"Don't go skating on Otter Creek, boys"
And we didn't listen to him, again.
Come on, let's get Tommy and go anyway.

Off we went to his house
Just three fun loving teenagers
not thinking about trouble, the "don't you go there"
or what lay ahead.

From shore the ice looked thick enough
so we bounded onto the frozen river
me on the old man's skates
Bill and Tommy riding their bikes.

Halfway out onto the ice
I looked down
and could see the water rushing beneath me.
Oh! Oh! I'm in trouble.

CRACK!
I fell through the ice and
wondered why the bike riders hadn't fallen in.
"Don't come after me," I shouted.

I crawled up on the ice
just like the Boy Scouts taught me
and started inching toward the bank.
believing I could make it to safety.

CRACK!
I went in again.

This time more scared than cold.
Once more I crawled out on the ice and headed for shore

CRACK!
Uh no! I don't know if I can make it.
yet I crawled up on the ice again
hoping my luck would hold out..

Finally I was close to shore and
you guys grabbed a stick and held it out to me.
Thank God I was out of the icy trap and on safe ground.
I would have been sweating bullets except I was frozen solid.

I know both of you got me back to Tommy's house
where his mother filled a tub with hot water and in I went.
As she searched for a big towel I heard her laughing,
"I think you boys are in big trouble."

How many times thereafter
did I skate on thin ice
and looking back on those dangers
remember surviving the challenge.

Expectation

Sleep wouldn't come that night
thoughts of Opening Day danced through his mind.
May 1st, trout season started in Vermont.
He didn't know it then,
but it was adrenaline that pumped through his body.
Again, the thrill that this time, he'd catch the elusive trout
stocked in Tenny Brook.
In his fitful sleep he could feel the tug on his line.
As the sun rose over the eastern mountains
he was full of excitement, knowing
today would be the day.

A short bike ride to Ma's best friend, Aunt Min.
Like Joey Chitwood he screamed into the driveway
threw down his kick stand,
said hi to Aunt Min and scrambled down the hill to the
    inviting brook.
He put the wiggling worm on the hook.
"Spit on it once for good luck," that's what the old man said.
"Throw it in the water." He could see the swirling mass in
    the pool.
Come on fishy fishy.

He walked up and down the stream with other kids.
Some had fish, most didn't.
But all were having fun,
enjoying the warm spring sun,
dreaming like Huck Finn and Tom Sawyer.
What a blessing those days were.

Still fishing sixty-five years later.
An older Tom or Huck,

standing in the rushing stream,
enjoying the experience of throwing a fly in the water,
The mountain sun warms his soul.
His only expectation is finding peace in the world.

On Becoming an Altered Boy

I am finally going to be special.
Sister Bridget is going to teach me Latin.
And then I will become an altar boy.
Hallelujah!
Ad Deum qui laetificat juventutem meam
"To God who gives joy to my youth"

Sister Bridget, was one of five Irish sibling Sisters of
    Saint Joseph.
She always had a smile and a patient attitude
as she wrote those unfamiliar words and phrases on the
    chalk board.
At times the long black sleeves of her habit would turn
    white from words she had written.
"Ok Timmy, repeat after me."
Being taught by Sister Bridget was not a chore to be endured,
but a special connection to the church.

Sister Bridget taught the ritual of the mass to the sponge
    like mind
that inhabited my brain.
She touched that deep part of me that still searches
 for that special connection between the words, the music
    and the rituals
that bring meaning to my life
Twenty seven years after I left my church,
I still miss the ritual and spirituality that came
from the teachings of Sister Bridget.

One Red, One Blue

Exiting the iron horse-
our matte black Buick sedan-
we were told to stay in the driveway.
Heads cocked, relying on sound
we tried to determine what was there.
The bright sun masked our vision,
hearts pounding like trip hammers
a warm breeze on our faces
there is no sound of danger.

For two weeks we had been at camp.
Away from familiar things,
the comfort of home,
a mother's meals,
the dos and don'ts
of everyday life.

It had been fun.
Rules, yes.
Swim with a buddy.
Take your turn.
Make your bed.

"Close your eyes."
We wondered what was next.
On a late July Sunday afternoon
like animals listening for a sound
we anticipated something
but didn't know what.
"OK, open your eyes."

Two brand new Wilson bicycles!
One Red, One Blue

Dunmore Fun

In Vermont springtime when the mountain roads were
    thawed and drivable,
word went out,
"Time to move to the lake."

My uncle Mike and aunt Dot owned a house on
    Lake Dunmore.
Their cabin at the southernmost tip of the lake sat high
    above the lakefront,
surrounded by tall pines whose needles over the years
created a soft carpet in the forest.
Silence was golden during the summer months, broken only
    by chirping of birds,
clicking of crickets and the laughter of teenagers playing.

Dot and Mike were stand-in parents for Billy and me.
Young teenagers then, too old for Camp Holy Cross, a
    Catholic camp.
So when Mom and Dad wanted to take a vacation
we were packed off to the lake.
Our only clothes were something clean for Sunday Mass,
bathing suits and sneakers.
We were taught the rules, but not the "thou shalt not" kind.
They were more like "that might not be a good idea."
The freedom we felt allowed us to explore different worlds.

Of course we had responsibilities.
If you take it out, put it back.
Clean up after yourself.
Keep the house neat, sort of.
Work with others.
But the first summer we were there Mike asked,

"How would you boys really like to help out?"
"Sure Mike," we said, "Whatever you need."
"How about painting the cabin this summer!!!"

We were up at dawn, bathing suits on, no shirts, ready to start.
Before Mike left for work he would give us specific
    instructions.
"This is the paint, these are the brushes, shake the can up
    real good.
It was bright red, smelly and sticky.
"Just paint this side today."

What did we know about painting?
But we got after it.
Brush in the can, wipe it off, slather it on the wood.

Lunchtime came, but Dot said we had to eat outside.
We were covered with paint.
But we did finish that side.

Then we had to clean up. What a sight we were.
There was not enough lava soap to remove the paint.
Turpentine, paint thinner, whatever it took. We finally
    cleaned up and were looking
only slightly red, more from the scrubbing than the paint.
We were proud of our work and couldn't wait for Mike to
    get home.

We rushed out to meet him and show off our painting skills.
While we stood there admiring our work, Mike snuck up
    behind us,
and painted big red stripes on our backs.
"Nice job boys."

And broke out into that big hearty laugh that followed Mike
    wherever he went.
What a picture the three of us were.
We loved Uncle Mike and would do anything for him.
So we painted again the next day.

The Fly Rod

The bamboo fly rod came with me from Vermont.
It rarely felt the pull of trout.
But there was a pull in my heart
that said it was an important part of my past.
Repairs were impractical,
so I hung it on the wall,
a reminder of something
stirring in the back of my mind.
It hung there every day
as if to say,
"Don't forget who you are."
I wanted to pass it on to my son,
but he said "no."
He didn't want it in his trophy room.
Cripes! Drive a stake in my heart!
So it went to the high bidder at a garage sale.
Part of me was lost that day.
But the memory of fly fishing will always be there.

Lost

Their last battle had been acrimonious and scathing.
The flames of anger licked at their souls.
The father told him to change his ways.
"Do what you're told, he said."
Even though near death, those words were swords slicing
 his son's heart.
But he fought back against the thrusting of the father's anger.
He said, "Who are you to tell me what to do?"
Unspoken words were "can't you see the good in me?"
The father's unspoken words "I love you."
The son had years of anger welling up in him.
He didn't know where it came from,
but it chewed at him like a snarling wolf.
There was a molten ball in his gut that wanted to retaliate.
The father was dying an easy target for the son.
Well, the son thought I came here to say goodbye.
So he kissed his father's forehead said he loved him then
 went for a drink.
Thirty days later the old man died and his son realized he
 could never go home again.

The Invisible Goddess

You were there for twenty-eight years.
And then you weren't.
What a void that left in my soul.

Your presence permeated my life
while you were here,
and continued long after you were gone.

Who you really were was a mystery to me.
I saw your outside, but your inside
remained buried in a shell of sorrow.

What a joy it would be to say, "Ma, I'm here."
And you would say, "Let's sit and have coffee."
I grieve the loss of sitting with you and sharing our stories.

Tied at the Hip

Your hold on me was like an invisible tether
that tied my soul to your hip.
I didn't know it was my job
to heal your hurt and fill your life.
I was just a kid when it was given to me.

Nobody gave me a set of rules.
Guilt washed over me when I didn't measure up.
Long after you were gone
I continued to say yes,
until one day I said no.

And then I was free.
That freedom was just the beginning of
finally understanding what you really needed.

A Lesson Not Learned

I remember the painful times in our lives.
Death took your younger brother,
your father, and a son.
Then your husband went off to war.
Your mother died. Two more brothers.
I don't ever recall seeing you grieve.
You must have learned to hide your anxiety.
I'm sorry to have missed that lesson.
You hid your life,
and in the process I learned to hide mine.

Long Ago Memories

I

After two years in the army
I walked up the porch steps,
dropped my duffel bag
and rang the bell.
Your smile a mile wide,
lit up my heart.
You had a bone crushing hug.
You said,
"Oh my baby boy is home.
I have missed you terribly."

The old man said,
"I didn't think you were coming until tomorrow."

II

I can't remember the sound of your voice,
the smell of your perfume or your laugh.
I do remember your cough.

"Don't smoke," you said.
But you smoked!

Money Doesn't Grow on Trees

"Dad, can I have fifteen dollars for a glove?
I want to learn how to play baseball,
and I don't have a glove.
The other guys have them. Huh, can I have a glove. Please?"

"Money doesn't grow on trees, son."
    Where does it grow. I'll go harvest some.

"I work hard for our money.
I go to the office every day and sweat and toil."
    It doesn't look like sweat and toil to me.
    You look pretty clean when you come home.

"Do you know how much it costs to pay our bills?"
    No! Do you think I learned finances in the seventh grade?

"Look at this check book.
This is not fun stuff."
    That checkbook looks like hen scratching to me.
    No wonder we don't have any money.

"I have to pay the mortgage and
groceries and utilities."
    Mortgage! What's that?

"We have to buy clothes for you and your brother."
    You pay money for these clothes?

"And pay for you to go to school."
    School should be free.

"We have to support our church,
so we can all go to heaven."
I'm not interested in heaven, Dad
I just want to learn how to play baseball.

A Letter I Never Received

March 24, 2017

Dear Tim,

Hopefully by the time you get this letter the Feral Pigs, aka, FPs
will be eradicated, as will their counterparts, the Russian Razorbacks.
Mr. Phluphyhead knew how to change the ordinary man into an FP.
He fed them with promises of power, birthday gifts every day of the year.
"You want it you got it," he told them.
No consequences. Really! Feral pigs don't care about consequences!
So they flocked to him when he said, "Here piggy-piggy."
"You will be great again."

Everyone ridiculed Phluphyhead. They said no way is he the one.
But, there he was, he crushed the pretenders and, then, "The Anointed One."
He moved into the People's House
without his current mate who stayed in the Tower.
He began to surround himself with the fatter and more voracious FPs.
Some had been hiding in public view.
Other names popped up, and we asked, "Where did they come from."

Phluphyhead believed the pen is mightier than the sword, hence, Executive Orders.

As he signed each one, he held up for the world to see.
Or maybe to say, "Look what I did Mommy, aren't I a
    good boy."

Every day, one of the lesser FPs came before the public to
    extol Phluphy's greatness.
He met with his perceived lessers of the world.
He instructed them on their responsibilities i.e. paying for
    the wall,
paying for our defense, giving our jobs back to us. Phluphy
    was so great!
It would be beautiful he said. You will love it.

If you are lucky Tim, Phluphy and his herd of FPs will be
    gone, wading in the waters of Mar-a-Lago
because, of course, global warming and climate change were
    not facts!

Hopefully,
Tim

The Journey Begins

Finally, the chance to leave home
Secretly he wanted to create a new self
to be his own person with
nobody telling him what to do

University of Vermont, Pre-Med
What a nice ring that had to it
He got lost in this new world
of chemistry, biology, algebra, trig

Then doubt began to enter his mind
Did he fit in? Could he fit in?
He changed majors, the easy way out.
Hi I'm a Poli Sci major and an SAE pledge

Panty raids, keg parties, road trips to Canada.
Fraternity parties would help him loosen up,
help him become one of the guys, except
most guys were smarter than him.

Next year will be better he thought
His parents said the military
would help him grow up.
Great, what a treat for Uncle Sam.

A sense of failure entered his soul
(and followed him for years.)
A lifetime of dreaming about tomorrow
became his way of dealing with life

Starting Anew

On a road taking him to a new life,
tears streamed down his cheeks
as the snow fell heavily on the Interstate.
The future looked foreboding as he thought
about everything he had lost.
He tried not to feel guilty.

Far from lifelong friends, church and beliefs
his sadness overwhelmed him and yet,
it was a choice he had to make.
His carried his grief like a heavy rock in his gut.
He drove to his new home in a truck
not his own, because like his marriage
it too was broken.

His children were angry.
His brother said,
"You are the good son. You can't do this."
His friends asked,
"couldn't you have done more to make it work?"
And when it seemed as if they all turned against him,
he started to turn from them.
And began burning some bridges.

Parking in the driveway of his new home, he unloaded
a desk, his daughter's dresser and his tools.
At least he could make a living.
What will I do he thought as he surveyed his new home.
The sadness and loss overcame him again.
It would take a long time to heal the anger and start
    rebuilding.

Washer, dryer, stove, refrigerator, warmth and a garage
    that he could lock.
I have everything I need he thought.
And then a sense of peace came over him.

Long Journey Home

I wanted to get into trouble
but not get caught
Something said
I had to be good little Timmy
Ma needed me to be her shield

I didn't want that job
Certainly, I didn't want to be sweet
I wanted to be like Billy
Chase girls, shoplift, hot wire cars
Be daring and take chances

But there it was, on my platter
I was formed early to be something other
than what I wanted to be
I played that role for awhile
But eventually it was time to fly away

Part of my soul left home one year
and it wandered far and wide
That painful journey led me into dark places
where I sought fulfillment for my fractured soul
I didn't know what I really wanted but the ache was ever
    present

I told the old man I was trying to find myself
"Find yourself, what the hell does that mean
Be a man, grow up...get a job."
A job...one of his answers to all my problems!

Then one day I looked into the abyss
and said, "No more. I am lost."

Gradually over time healing began
The fear that woke me every morning
slowly began to disappear with the rising sun

Over time I faced my painful past
and my true self began to appear
Like spring snow the dark side slowly melted
and my shadows became visible
Baffling dreams became clear and eventually
Timmy was healed and I appeared.

Alone in the World

"Are you going to work on our marriage," she shouted.
He knew there was no easy answer to that question.

He felt lost in this dark wilderness,
and feared what would come next.
"There is nothing more I can do," he said softly.

"Do you want a divorce," she screamed at him.
Finally, the ball was in his court, his choice.
From deep within came what needed to be said. "Yes"!
For many years "Yes" lay buried
in an impasse of his fear, uncertainty and *what ifs*.

"Get out of my house," she shouted at him.
"You call my parents and tell them,
call your brother and tell him,
call our children and tell them."

Her anger was white hot
and fearful to face.
Even though there was doubt in his mind
his heart said this was the right choice.

His children were angry and wouldn't speak to him.
His brother said
"You are the good son. You can't do this."
His friends asked,
"Couldn't you have done more to make it work."

And when it seemed as if they had all turned against him,
and he could find no find solace in his church,
he started to turn from them.
Then a deep sadness filled his heart.

Forgiveness

His insides were raw on the treacherous roads he travelled
Despair and fear were his constant companions.
He finally admitted,
"I am so lost and weary, overwhelmed with sorrow.   Please.
    Forgive me."

"I do," said the spirit.

Forgiveness came.
Like a warm blanket it healed his burning soul.
Rekindled the love he extinguished
all those years ago when he said "NO!"
Peace finally entered his world.
The slate was clean.

"Who am I now?" he asked.
"You are the one you were meant to be" said the spirit.
Follow your true path back home.

Anger Released

The snarling beast
awoke that morning
pondering the shattered dreams at his feet
wondering if his ruptured life would ever heal
A cauldron of simmering anger
bubbling to the surface
    Nobody ever listened to him
    Not even you god.

You were absent when he needed you god
Your bible bullshit and church rules
left him empty and desolate
Men are not supposed to feel as he did
they said suck it up brother
be a man
    "I was dying inside
    and you turned your back on me."

The snarling bear drew his claws back
grabbed the hammer and slammed the floor
anger flowing through his arms
sweat dripping from his scalp
hands pained from the pounding
like molten lava years of anger poured forth from his soul
    "Damn it
    where were you"

Exhausted he lay on the dirty floor
Surely, therapy would have been easier
but anger was such a familiar tool
it had lain simmering beneath his skin
and now it was out, it was ok

he was not struck dead
    In that exhaustion came relief
    and he could find gratitude for the God
    who had always been there

The Reluctant Learner

Heading out alone was the way to peace
I didn't know I was a loner
and withdrew because
only my space felt safe

In my teens I was an inexperienced
and poorly outfitted skier
Yet I was drawn to that place
where I felt the most insecure

My companions said
follow us if you want to learn
So I did
I fell, got up, returned and didn't quit

I learned to start over after my mistakes
In time I became my own skier
and found satisfaction in solitude
where the environment was my friend.

The Creature Within

Who is this creature that still rumbles around in my soul.
"I am in you and you are in me, and God is in both of us,"
    it says.
But why the hell does the son-of-a-bitch still hang around?

Who are you?
You look like the little sneak in the Lord of the Rings.
You are a dishonest son of a bitch troublemaker.
You don't speak the truth.
You try to drag me back to a world full of resentment, anger
    and fear.
What am I not getting that prevents me from letting you go?

Are you hurting that bad?
Do you need to be loved?
Do you need to be loved into existence?
I don't know how to let you go.

I want to grab you by the throat and throw you off the cliff,
yet I know I need to love you.
Who can love a slimy beast like you?
I want to pound you in the head,
yet I need to love you.
How do I do that?

We Are One

Spring Break 1964

As he rides to the top his mind wanders.
What trail first.
Which will be the most challenging.
How hard does he want to push himself.
He is invigorated. The cold enters his body.
The eastern sun at his back
outlines his shadow on the snow covered trees.
When he sees the top the adrenaline energizes him.

The panorama of the mountains stirs his soul.
Peaks of five mountain ranges spread out before him.
He feels free in this snow-covered playground.
The only boundaries are the ones he creates.
He can be himself
Free to take chances
Free to fail, get up and start again.

He begins the heart pounding descent.
Flying over some moguls, swooshing around others.
The challenge of the trail makes his heart sing.
He is exhilarated by the cold burning his face.
Even as his knees ache
he persists.

Snow covered pines rush by him. He is fearless.
He and the mountain are brother and sister.
His center comes up though the earth's crust and the snow.
"Today I am free to be me."

Joy Lost and Maybe Found

I wake up one morning
and realize that joy is no longer in my soul.
Just another retirement day.
Where did the joy go?
Like a shadow in moonlight it disappeared.
What comes next?
Should I start leaving a written legacy?
Plan my funeral? Write the obituary?
Where the hell is the joy in that.
Yet I know those things need to happen.

This morning, awake before I want to get up,
I thank God for another day.
My feet hurt so I don't want to stand.
But when I look in the mirror and shave I think,
"not bad looking for an old guy."
I look at me and say, "Be happy knucklehead."
Enjoy the day, enjoy the challenges,
enjoy the opportunities.
I see the sun, the flowers, the little old ladies walking
their dogs. I watch parents walking their children
to school. Now that is joyful.

Forget the damned politicians.
I'll look for the little things that bring joy and happiness
to my world. The smile that is on Beverly's face
every morning. The first ray of sunshine.
Now that is joy.

Taking Chances

Adventure isn't hanging on a rope off the side of a mountain.
Adventure is an attitude that we must apply
to the day-to-day obstacles of life.
John Amatt

They were two travelers from different worlds.
both seeking peace and acceptance.
With apprehension, they shed their pasts
to move forward

Somewhere deep in their souls
a spark glowed that said,
you will be ok.
Don't look for the ideal
just see what each day brings.
Then grab the opportunity.

The mentor said,
We are volunteers here and will
learn to sit with others in their
challenging times. We will also
learn about each other.

The spark glowed brighter for this couple.
And hope was reborn in them.

Opening Doors

Effective communication starts with listening.
Robert Gately

The sofa was uncomfortable,
so they sat on the floor.
They ate pizza, watched March Madness
and talked about stuff.

"Tell me about it," she asked.
And with that graceful invitation,
doors that were closed for so long
slowly began to open.

Parents, high school, college,
marriage, children, divorce,
religious beliefs, friends.
New worlds opened between them
offering opportunities for trust, acceptance and growth.

Listening was the foundation
that made it safe sharing their stories.
The painful pasts were given light
in the protected space between them.
The unveiling of secrets created a bond that drew them closer.

Late Life Love

Adrenaline pumping through his veins,
his loins on fire...heart racing with excitement.
Is this really love when he is hot and ready to roll?
Come on baby, I love you," he says, *honest I do!"*
Then the explosion and the fire goes out.
Ashes left in the pit of his stomach and in his mouth.
Next...!

"Come on baby," he says. *"I need some loving."*
Not tonight honey, I'm tired. Maybe tomorrow,
the kids have me worn out."
"Don't you love me anymore?"
"Yes, but..."
They have kids, work and a mortgage to pay.
He struggles with understanding love in those times.
Some of the fire is there, but also something else.

And then the kids are gone.
They are alone again, and some of the old fire returns.
But, it is different this time.
A comfortable nurturing love sprouts and takes flight.
His heart is committed to their marriage.
Together they feel the silent love in the room.
Despite challenges, their love continues to grow.
This late life loving is best for feeding their souls.
It is life giving.

Gardening

At the heart of gardening, there is a belief in the miraculous.
         Mirabel Osler

The garden blooms because of their love.
Blossoms and new growth abound
and feeds their souls.
Just as the garden needs to be tended, so do they.
And it is done with love and tenderness.
If the soil of the home is fertile,
love grows and weathers the storms of life.

Healing At The Kitchen Sink

I stood there,
feeling the shame of a life filled with supposed sins.
I am no good.
I am not worthwhile.
I don't know what the sin was, but it said,
you are not worth a damn.
SHAME ON YOU, SHAME ON YOU!!
Can't you ever get it right?
What a stupid boy you are, AGAIN.
I stood at the sink, my head bowed, tears streaming down
    my face.
The shame was like a molten rock in my gut.
Is there no hope for me?

I could feel her presence there,
She wrapped her arms around my dejected body and said I
    love you.
That closeness helped me shed the flayed skin that I wore.
Hope came alive for me with that touch.
There is one person in this world who thinks I am worthwhile.
Maybe in time there will be two of us.
That touch opened the door to healing a lifetime of shame.

New Year's Stir Fry

This was the end of my first
solitary year in twenty-five years.
I wondered what Beverly was planning.
Do you have plans for New Year's Eve?
What the heck, jump in, take a chance.

I don't know why I said,
Do you want to come over
to my place? I'll do stir fry.
I owned a frying pan, one or two
spoons and forks and confidence
in my one dish.

Beverly drove to my place.
Concrete floors, venetian blinds,
a fifty dollar sofa bed, and a
TV with a disappearing picture,
And...hope?

I knew how to paint and cook
stir fry. I was learning how
to be social and to trust.
So I told her more of my story.

Page by page we went through
my year books. I showed her my
family pictures.
She took it all in
accepting me as I was.
It felt safe being with Beverly.

Then it was midnight.
Happy New Year.
Time for Beverly to go home.
   "Thanks for coming."

How was I supposed to know she wanted a kiss.

The First Kiss

(Another night of TV and pizza.)
"Tell me about you." she says
"Who are you? What's important in your life?"
I answer, "Peace, acceptance, forgiveness."

Time to leave again.
A goodbye hug on the stairs.
(Don't want her to get a stiff neck.)

A longer hug leads to the first kiss and,
"I love you."
(O boy! What will I do now?)
Do I want to keep that door open?

The M Word

Another Saturday road trip.
Off to Holdenville to visit grandmother.
Shawnee for a BBQ lunch and then
a side trip to Meeker.

Conversation, a deal breaker in the past,
comes easier for him now.
He shares more of his past and expectations,
and she listened with an open heart.

Then he dives in and says,
"Should we be talking about the "M" word?"
Wow! He just plunged into serious territory.
Was he ready for marriage again?

There was no anxiety, so
the future was explored.
It felt like the time was right.
They knew who they were.
Trust and acceptance had been created.

Hope Lives

From the minute the pathologist issued the warning
to put her affairs in order,
their hearts had been shattered.
Over lunch they calmly tried to talk about the future,
but there it was,
she might die this year.

As they entered the atrium that housed her oncologist's office
a proud bald woman strode defiantly into their lives.
She filled that cold space with hope.
Wearing sunlit colors with a multicolored turban,
and gold sparkling hoop earrings,
she smiled as if she were winning the war.
What magnificent courage they thought.

Waiting for the doctor and an uncertain future,
the thought ran through their minds,
"just maybe."
Until he walked into the room and said
"My name is Dr. Geister and
I have good news."

Home

There is beauty all around when there is love at home.
Anonymous

We don't have stuff in our home.
What you see is an expression of who we are.

Tim Reardon
July 19, 2017

Overs

Even before,
"Do you think we could go out sometime,"
trust and safety drew this wounded couple together.
There were no expectations,
just company for the passage of time.

Their stories and March Madness
brought them closer together.
In time hope appeared on the horizon.
Then a stairway hug led to a kiss,
which led to an "I love you" and the beginning of their
    commitment.

Facing the second half of their lives
they looked to the future with hope.
Experienced travelers now, and
aware of storms that lay in their path,
they joined hands with joy.

They lived lovingly and intentionally
as they held each other's hearts with an
"I love you" in the morning and
"I love you" in the evening.
Like a Fabergé' Egg their love was priceless.

Their playful loving ways
brought out the children in them.
Explosions of Sunday morning love and caramel rolls allowed
a freedom they had never known.
They became as one in those times.
"Do we have to go to church this morning?"

Eventually, storms appeared on the horizon.
"We have each other's back"
was a bulwark against these storms.
Living one day at a time,
they grew spiritually and emotionally.

Their wedding vows were lived each day
and became who they were.
As they entered the fourth quarter
their love continued to grow,
their lives prospered, and they shared their love with others.

Goodbye Sweetie

The hard part was leaving his "Sweetie."
They have lived together
one day at a time for over 25 years
The sadness of his early departure
felt like a shroud on his heart

He was sad she would wake up one morning and not hear
"Good morning Sweetie. I love you."
They had nurtured each other
while settling in to living
with fatal diseases

Initially, they purchased nothing new
Lifetime guarantees were a joke
Through children and grandchildren problems,
family illnesses and death
their partnership became stronger

Even though they were at an in-between space again
they found ways to support each other in their daily journeys
They did not give up
They continued to flourish

The Midnight Bandit

What is this darkness
that wakes me at night?
No name, no shape
just an invisible shroud.

It steals my well being
and stays with me until early morning
I have a one-sided conversation with it
Who are you? Why are you here?

The lack of an answer leaves me feeling empty
and steals the joy I seek.
I am not ready for the day
with this gloom hanging over me.

Does this pall foreshadow my death?
Am I at peace with my future?
I want to find joy every day.
How do I shake this stalker?

Another Bullet

Twenty-one years ago
he looked death in the eye
and said "I am not afraid."
And here it was again
knocking on his door

Another bullet to dodge
Pulmonary Fibrosis…Incurable, maybe treatable,
the best result is to die with it, not from it
"What the hell does that mean."
He struggled with his new challenge

He had much to finish
story telling, drawing, writing
yet he didn't see himself finishing anything
When he went he wanted a pen in his hand
or a club yelling "Fore"

He knew how to live one day at a time
with an undefined future and accept what is
He knew where to look for the possibilities
and not be afraid today
He understands acceptance.

The hard part was leaving his "Sweetie."
They have lived together
one day at a time for over 25 years
The sadness of his early departure
was like a shroud on his heart

He was sad that Beverly will wake up and not hear
"Good morning Sweetie. I love you."

They had nurtured each other
while settling in to living
with fatal diseases

Initially, they purchased nothing new
Lifetime guarantees were a joke
Through children and grandchildren problems
and family illnesses and death
their partnership became stronger

They supported each other in their daily journeys.
and never gave up
Even though they were at an in-between space
They still felt useful
They would continue to grow.

Scarred

Scarred lungs, scarred life.
Taking too many wrong turns
had tempted the gods for a long time
First, a cigarette...because his parents said no
Then, the first drink...because something said it would
    make him whole
Physical and emotional injuries piled up over the years

It wasn't the physical scarring that hurt him the most
His damaged body healed...somewhat
It was the scarred soul
that took forever work
Where does one start when he says,
no more...somebody please help me.

The soul doesn't heal by itself.
There is no salve for that scarring .
There is no magic potion that will heal others
It comes from the hard work of asking forgiveness
seeking humility, reaching out for help and saying
I cannot walk this healing road alone

Under Seige

The painful pressure startles him from a deep sleep.
Not now he thinks as he rationalizes about his "heartburn."
He has too much going on for this to happen.
Guilt gnaws at him.
knowing he did a lousy job protecting his heart.

Sneaks a nitro, goes back to bed
Five minutes and the monster is back.
"Damn I don't have time for this crap."
Pops another nitro, goes back to bed.
Another five minutes, another nitro then
    "Beverly Call 911!"

The iron band becomes tighter around his chest,
and the monster says, "I'm back baby!"
He moans and buckles over as the pressure increases.
His son, visiting from out of town,
watches helplessly his father struggle for life.

"I'm sorry for upsetting everyone."
"God," he thinks, "I don't have time for this."
Too much going on.
More important things to do.
Home opener tomorrow.

By now he has moved to the living room.
There is no room for a gurney in the bedroom.
"On a scale of one to ten how bad is the pain,"
"Eleven" as he moans and grabs his chest again
"have taken three nitro, no relief."

Finally EMSA shows up!
He asks for a Ziploc for his medicine.
They'll want to know what he takes.

The pain in his chest is agonizing.
He feels scared and helpless in the hands of the gods.
The medics wrap him in warm blankets,
and load him into the ambulance.
As he starts to go into shock,
they spray nitro in his mouth.
Beverly wants to know if she can ride with them.
Not a good idea they tell her.
She feels deserted as they speed away.

Sirens blaring the ambulance screams down May Avenue.
I might die tonight he thinks
and in his delirium realizes,
all is well with his soul,
he is willing to let go.
As he drifts in and out of consciousness
a sense of peace settles over him.

The emergency room doctor tells him he has a major blockage.
"You can clear it with drops or we can insert a needle."
Taking the easy way out "I'll take the drops."
The cardiologist says "You are in deep trouble my friend.
I would insert a needle."
"Ok, but do it quick."
Finally there is relief then sleep.

He wakes the next morning struggling for breath.
Oxygen in his nose, needles in his arms.
His chest feels like it was hit with a sledge hammer.
He realizes the pearly gates were open last night,

and fortunately closed just before he arrived.
"I'm sorry I did this on your birthday, Beverly."

He wants to know what to do with the football tickets for today's game.

He still struggles with getting priorities straight.

Doctor

Accept my body. Please.
I give it freely.
Honor me by letting it
be your teacher.
I am humbled to be here.
My spirit will bless your work and,
I know you will respect me,
so I fear not.

The first time you see me,
really see me, be inquisitive.
You may ask, "who was this man?"
Your journey of exploration will reveal the physical me.
And my family will tell you about my spiritual journey.
The damaged heart in your hand represents my soul,
which in a sometimes torturous lifetime
had been transformed into a man of peace.
I shared my life with others.
I hope my final gift
will encourage you to do the same.

He Is Disappearing

Cancer! Multiple Myeloma! Chemotherapy!
I didn't even know what those words meant.
The old man looked fairly healthy.
His acerbic tongue again was there.
And I was his target.
But something was different.
I began to realize he was dying.
And a dark shadow covered my soul.

It had been a year since we crossed swords,
so when I walked in the door I was stunned.
The bones of a once vibrant man, protruding like toothpicks,
were covered with graying skin like parchment.
Sparse white hair that once barely covered his head
had disappeared.
Who was this person?

He had always been healthy.
Strong hands and heart toiled to improve the health
of his patients. He hummed and whistled while he worked.
Sarcasm, although hurtful at times,
left me in stitches at others.
He threw a 15# bowling ball down the alley every
    Wednesday night,
and taught me to do the same.
We tramped the Vermont woods in the fall looking for grouse.
Didn't shoot many, but he exposed me to the beauty of nature.
Unsuccessfully he showed me how to fish.
Yet I still enjoy throwing a fly in a cold mountain stream.

 He was like a little boy when the nurse picked him up.
She cradled him like he cradled me all those years ago.

Something left me that day, and I knew
I would never see him again as he once was.

Disappearing Friends

<u>Ron</u>

Like elementary students they lined up for lunch.
Some held hands, some didn't.
Wheelchairs, walkers, canes, and the ambulatory
Ron was the first one I recognized.

I said "Hi Ron," but there was no response,
just a ghostlike stare into another world
that only he inhabited.
And one that was safe for the time being.

I didn't know about his condition
but it put a chill in my heart.
Ron was younger than me.
A year later he was gone.

<u>Richard M, PhD</u>

He is Dickie to us
A fun loving quipster
who makes all his neighbors laugh.

At the Halloween party
he is the Sheik of Araby
resplendent in silken garb

He is always the first
to shout "BINGO"
when only three numbers have been called.

He loves to shop for groceries
without a list or menu in mind
and without his credit card

Love for
this childlike man
fills our hearts

<u>Jack</u>

College educated, athletic, hard working
successful businessman, leader in his church,
epitome of the Baby Boomer's dream

He stood tall in a world
where he was a problem solver
until something began to slip away

What am I eating for breakfast
What should I wear today
Where are my clothes

Don't tell me what to do
I want my damn car keys
Don't treat me this way.

Please don't leave me
I promise not to do it again.
I will do better

And the next morning
he is back to his new normal and
forgets what happened the day before.

Mark

Tour player, Ryder Cup Champion
Course designer and teacher
A humble man with a dry sense of humor
Always ready to help someone.
"You could keep doing it your way Robin,
or you might try this," he said with a sly smile

His muscle memory
drove the ball to the green.
Once there he was lost
He picked the ball up
put it in his pocket
and returned to the cart.

"Hit the ball, Mark."
He struck it like the pro he had been
but something silent was missing in that swing
A cloud of sadness grew in this threesome
as they watched their partner and friend disappear
They knew the final 19th green was approaching.

In Memory of my Friend Hyla

I know you are there,
waiting to pick my bones.
I hear the swoosh of your wings
and feel air rustling in my ears.
It is not my time.
There is football to watch,
food to share,
stories to tell
Go away! I'll tell you when!

What a struggle to live today,
 I'm not ready to quit,
even as I feel myself disappearing
in the presence of friends.
They see me here,
yet know I am slowly passing to the other side.
I see their sadness in their eyes and want to comfort them.

The fire I carried all those years is being suffocated.
I am losing the strength to fight; ready to accept the
      journey's end.
It is time to go.
Not Yet! Not yet!
Yes! Time for me to go.

Your darkening presence permeates my home.
I can hear the feather light tapping of your fingers on the door,
and the shuffling of your slippers on the carpet.
I hear the soft whispers of those around me.
They kiss me and say goodbye.
I am at peace as I leave this home.

Servants

The trio of elders sat in the gloomy room
This sacred space was filled with holiness
and love between these servant brothers
It was a bittersweet time.

Coming from different backgrounds
they found unity in service to the poor
Today two of them came here
to break bread with the one
who could no longer serve

"Are we ready to eat?"
"Can we pray?"

"Heavenly Father, we are grateful for your presence.
We thank you for the life of our friend John
for everything he did to serve our country and those in need
We ask that you give him strength for his journey
We know you have blessed him and his work
and his presence has blessed us."

There was no idle chatter between these friends
as they ate and reminisced about what brought them
    together.
Laughing, they recalled problems created and solved.
Each man knew some hidden power
deep in their souls drew them together.

When the meal had been eaten
and leftovers put away, they said their goodbyes.
 "It was good to see you again, John."
But what was left unsaid filled the room.

Lunch at Ables

As we walked out of the collectible shop I asked
"Where is a good place to eat lunch in these parts."
(I didn't want to sound too much like we came from the
    big city.)
"Back up the road through two lights on the right
    hand side."
We pulled in to an almost empty parking lot.
Well he said it was good.

The sign said "Wait to be seated."
That seemed unusual for a place that was nearly empty.
Only one table to the right had any diners seated.
It looked like they were all eating the Monday special,
Rib dinner, beans, slaw and roll. $8.79
They were chompin' down like there was no tomorrow.
They looked like regulars and seemed to be friends.

We ordered burgers and fries and ice tea. Delicious!
Six men came through the door and filled the room with
    their presence.
They sure weren't lawyers!
You could tell they were hard working men, big rough,
    cracked hands.
Shirts hanging out, boots covered with mud,
Smiling and apparently happy men who looked like they
    were lifelong friends.
You would think they'd order beer by the gallon, but instead
    they had sweetened iced tea.

Others kept flowing in. We were lucky to beat the lunch sit
    down and take out crowd.

Six young men, probably 30 years younger than the old guys
    came in and set up a table for themselves.
They were all friends breaking bread together, sharing
    community.
We wondered about the education level, the earnings and
    the healthcare
in this small town.
Do they really think Washington cares about people in
    Antlers, Oklahoma?

It seemed like being in Abel's brought everything down to
    the basics.
Good friends, good food, hard work.
What a great lunch.

The Silent Minority

These brown skinned laborers from other countries
Can be seen at the 7-11.
They buy enough food for a day's hard labor in the hot sun.
Burritos, tamales, water bottles, ice chests full.
They are roofers, gardeners and landscapers.

Smiling and chatting they visit with one another,
I try to make eye contact and smile
but they turn away. I am not one of them.

As the sun is rising they are on the roof
Shovels out, tearing off old shingles.
Or in the garden digging holes for new plants.
Scurrying back and forth they know their jobs.

Their chatter is constant.
Smiling and laughing they seem to be energized by hard, physical labor.
Noon comes and they break for lunch under a friendly shade tree.
Do they talk about their families, homes, those they left behind?
Are they hoping for a better life, worried about ICE*?

Back on the burning roof in the afternoon sun
or in the garden spreading mulch, the chattering continues.
These diligent workers stay until their tasks are finished.
They are gone before I can thank them.

Immigration Customs and Enforcement

For Our Friend Peri Ann

Were you there God when Perry got sober?
When he said "I can't live this way.
No more God, please help me."

Were you there God when Peri Ann said "I am not a he but
 a she?"
Did you hold her hand while she transitioned?
"No more God, please help me."

Were you there God when Peri Ann lay broken beneath
 that truck?
Did you hold her in your arms as she passed over?
Were you really there God? Assure us she didn't die alone.

We look for a "why" God.
We want an answer.
But maybe the why is not important

Perhaps the answer comes when
we sit in grieving circles and talk about the who.
The Peri Ann who courageously walked and shared her story.

About others she carried in their journeys.
About how our lives have been changed.
And then we realize that Peri Ann will always be with us.

Someone Else's Child

This bundle of joy filled our sacred space with her beauty.
Garbed in what appeared to be a family heirloom
she was surrounded by a congregation of love.
We were there to accept her into our lives,
to offer protection in the storms ahead,
to share the collective wisdom of our beliefs
and to support her courageous parents on their journey.

Robin held her up for all to see.
Oohs and aahs bounced off the walls.
"What will this child be called," he asked.
"Eliza Rose Taylor,"
Responded Caitlin and Alan.
Turning to the congregation Lori asked,
"Since there is no such thing as someone else's child,
Will you be responsible for Eliza?"
"We will," they said enthusiastically.

Robin blessed Eliza in the sacred tradition of our church,
kissed her as only a grandfather could
and welcomed her into our flock.
A loud cheer went up in the sanctuary.

Thanksgiving At The Farm

There are traditions that go back in time
to when storytelling was important.
When clans gathered around camp fires and said
Once upon a time...
The Cain Gatherings have followed those traditions

In late fall Michael opens his door
And everyone is welcome
Friends and family come from near and far and
the hand of friendship is extended
to all who come into the glow of this hospitality

The prosperity that is shared today
comes from humble beginnings.
Howard and Ruth live on in the stories
shared by the elders
and by the stories told about trips to Holdenville.

New stories will be told about
the potato peeling contest—eyes in or out
and the building of the great pond
about trips to Padre and the unending search
for treasures in the sand

There will be legal disputes about guilt and innocence
and remembrances of wrestling in younger days
and challenges to get in shape for the next race
Is there enough firewood, what's the correct way to build
    a fire
All the while hearts are warmed through the gathering
    of family

When the meal is prepared everyone will gather
and give thanks for the blessings family
has received and for the love and acceptance
this family offers to all.

Company Rules

Rule # One: THE BOSS IS ALWAYS RIGHT!

The Pink Painter with his high school workers,
 a fun group to share time with during the summer.
There was Biff, Spider and Stumpy.
They were good for the boss.
An opportunity to chill out,
stop being anal, laugh once and awhile.
And every now and then laugh at himself.

They were trained to work hard all day.
Nose to the grindstone, be neat, no paint on the carpet,
cover the furniture,
no ma'am, yes ma'am to the homeowner.

"Biff, you and Spider start upstairs in the bedrooms.
Stumpy will work with me."
They mixed up the paint and got after it.
They took a break for lunch and then started again.
Stumpy and the boss painted the large living room.
It seemed like they almost didn't have enough paint, but
It looked great when they finished.
They cleaned up everything.
When Biff and Spider came downstairs they were shocked.
"That's the wrong color boss"!
"Why didn't you say something Stumpy"?

"Rule # One boss"

On Finding Peace

You asked how can one live at peace in a violent world
I ask how are you contributing to that violence
Non-violence requires a double faith, faith in God and also
    faith in man.

You asked how can I see us all as one
I ask when will you stop looking in the mirror
The best way to find yourself is to lose yourself
in the service of others.

You asked what did it feel like to speak truth to power
I ask what did it feel like to protest the death penalty
Strength does not come from physical capacity.
It comes from an indomitable will.

Everything you are looking for
is already inside you
The good man is the friend of all living things.

Follow Georgia O'Keefe's mantra

I decided to start anew
to strip away all that I had been taught
and accept as true my own thinking.
From Gandhi

My Own Paradise Lost

This fluid warms and protects me.
It is so safe here.
Everything I need for life;
nourishment, oxygen and warmth surround me.
Sometimes the world is still, other times not so much.
This person who carries me struggles with life.
There are two others out there who need her attention, one
    more than the other.
I am the only one here.
Why do I have to share her with the others.
 I need all of her.

Don't Tread On Me

I'm hiding in the rocks,
in the underbrush,
in the sunshine.
Sometimes you know I am there,
but not always. "Are you Ok?" she asks.

"Sure, nothing is wrong. I'm fine."
But there I slither,
waiting to strike.

*"Stay the hell away from me.
Stop whining.
Don't piss me off.
Somebody will get bitten today,
and I don't want it to be you."*

Who is this poisonous viper in the grass,
coiled and ready to strike.
Why does he want to do that?
I don't think he does, but there is still a sore in his soul
that has not healed. The viper stays hidden in the rocks.

*How will I heal that weeping sore
that seeks to destroy my life.*

Is This Football or What

Season opener is one week away,
and our group has changed.
I can see them now sixteen years ago.
They were looking for new blood.
Beverly and I were were it.

Game by game, we came to know them.
The librarian and story teller brought
good hearted humor to this group of friends.
His vegetarian wife brought her own food to the game,
and when the librarian departed she brought a new guy,
    a Yankee.

The architect-golfer was also an oil painter.
Our electrician saw the signing
of the Japanese surrender in Tokyo Bay.
His wife was one of the gourmet chefs in our group.
All I wanted was a hot dog.
She gave us meals from Bon Appetite.

One of the older ones
played tennis three days a week,
his other half gathered political pictures
for their refrigerator. OBAMA for President.

The male half of the urban farmers and game keepers
thought the game was over by the 3rd quarter.
They always royally entertained on New Year's Eve,
and usually got us home before ten.

The Adlerian philosopher sat in the corner observing.
We never knew what went on

in his deep well of thought.
His partner filled the void left by his silence.
She loved any challenge thrown her way.

Overlooking everyone was the Weather Goddess.
She could hold her own with everyone and we knew she
    loved us all.
We wondered where was the common ground.
I thought we liked football, but generally it's politics.

Some watched football, but their real fire was politics.
Yellow dog democrats and Hillary to the core.
When death intruded, we began to see the deeper
    connections.
There was a true lifelong love in this group.
Our hearts overflowed with gratitude because we were
    part of it.
The passing of the Weather Goddess showed us more than
    football held us together.

Winter Golf

There is a light wind blowing out of the south
Layered four times over against the cold
with gloves on both hands
he gathers with his friends on #1

"Ok, let's get started."
His back and feet ache, his hands sting from the cold
as he eyes the ball, swing…crack
Straight down the right side of the fairway.
"Wow, that's the way to start."

Fingers burning from the cold
he plays on
Some holes good, some not
two pars, two bogeys, some whatever.
He still enjoys the challenge of golf.

And then it's #10.
The wind becomes stronger
but the sun warms his back
"Damn," he says "79 years old
playing golf with friends in 41 degree temperature."
He is energized by this experience.

They finally finish eighteen holes.
Beaten down by the wind and cold
they are ready to get relief from the weather.
"Wow! This was great today
Same time next week?"

The Pied Piper and Feral Pigs: A Fable

O! Woe is us
Our town is full of feral pigs
Whatever shall we do they moaned
Surely there's a pig catcher somewhere

Who is this rescuer we seek
He's the Pied Piper who lives in the forest
He rides from town to town
eliminating the evil pigs

Will he help us get rid of evil in our village
For the right price he will do anything
Then contact this savior right away
We are buried in the offal of the feral pigs

Contact was made
Rid our town of feral pigs
and we will pay you a princely sum
The contract was signed and the Piper went to work

Within days the rooting creatures were gone
and the townspeople were overjoyed
When the Piper came for payment they reneged
Read the fine print etc. etc. etc. they said

Hell hath no fury like a Piper scorned
so within days he came back
sought out the not so feral pigs he missed
and piped them all into the river

Moral: Hopefully sooner or later the true pigs will be removed.

A Dreadful Mourning

What am I guilty of...*Again*
What have I done wrong...*Again*
What have I forgotten to do...*Again*

What is this dark cloud that hangs over me
Are there secrets that need to be revealed
Is there more to my story

Am I still a bad boy...*Again*

I never see myself as a bad man
Maybe my story is about mourning
   the part of me that has not mourned properly
   the part of me that has not mourned enough

The Hidden Hero's Journey

Children should be seen and not heard Timothy!
Don't speak until you're spoken to Timothy!
Wait your turn Mr.Reardon!
Each phrase burned into his soul, until,
He didn't know who he was or who he wasn't.

He wanted to ask her to dance.
Damn, just once let him ask her to dance!
"Don't speak until you're spoken to Timothy."
How WILL they know him if.....
"Children should be seen and not heard Timothy."
"He can get the job done boss," he said.
"Wait your turn Mr. Reardon."
His true self is covered with convention and rules
and in the box thinking.
He is shriveling up like a prune.
"Why do you want to be different Timothy"?
Because who he is,
is not who he wants to be.

He longed for the persona of Yosemite Sam,
that blustery, full steam ahead,
go to hell with convention Sam.
Guns blazing, smoke coming out of his ears,
scowling, scary eyes,
not aware of the mistakes in the road Yosemite Sam.
Either lead, follow or get the hell out of the way Sam.

He doesn't know you are buried deep in the cave of his soul.
Help him find release Sam.
Let him make enough of his own mistakes,
until he says,
what the hell I'm in trouble anyway.

And then he realizes people
laugh at his mistakes,
And not at him.
He takes on the characteristics of Yosemite Sam,
and becomes comfortable with the release he finds.
And then a new character emerges:
Mr. Bluster!

Mr. Bluster is his protector in vulnerable times.
When he is angry and lost Mr. Bluster
brings out the coat of armor.
Mr. Bluster is his constant companion,
until that time when he realizes Mr. Bluster
is not serving his best interests.
He realizes his shadow works against him and so,
the dark side of Mr. Bluster changes to an
engaging, inquisitive man,
one always ready to ask,
"Okay, who wants to dance"!

This Aquarius Male

January 20 - February 18

In this time of your life you are becoming aware of new ways
   to explore your creativity.
You are looking at the past and determining,
what is useful and what is not.

You will find ways to still your heart and look deep within
   your shadow.
Somewhere there are places that are not healed,
and through your poetry and story telling you will find them.
You will find forgiveness and acceptance in your journey.
You will find safe places to share your story
and you will draw to you those who follow a similar path.
You will be a spiritual friend to them as you both grow
   together.

Spring

A light cool breeze on my face.
The sun is warm on my back-
a wonderful afternoon
What a wonderful afternoon.
After the treacheries of winter
daffodils burst forth from the earth,
forsythia begins to bud and flower,
hew yellow petals adding glory to my world.
What a treasure spring is to me.
Everything lives in the dark until it is time to shoot forth.
After seventy eight years I am reborn.
I feel new growth in the dark soil of my soul.
I am fed in the darkness.
New growth waiting to spring forward,
new energy in my old bones.
I am alive again. This is my favorite time of year.
I loved springtime in my youth.
The snow capped peaks melting, created streams.
Fresh, cold, clean water.
New life, anticipation, hopes and dreams.
I am young again.

A Mother's Sadness

Joy and sadness filled her young heart
at the birth of the savior Son
She watched him suckling at her virgin breast
knowing he would follow His appointed path
just as she had followed hers.

Was he the Messiah, a prophet, or a teacher?
Whatever the choice
she knew the challenges he faced
would fill her heart with pain

The virgin mother wanted him to follow the appointed path,
yet ached to keep Him close to her
Sorrowfully, though, she
watched with love as His ministry began.

There were many followers who loved her son,
but there were others who despised Him and His work
He was going against the grain. Knowing this,
his mother's pain increased because she sensed the outcome.

And it came.
When he died on the cross.

What about the reality of Christ's physical suffering,
lashes by the Roman whip master,
punctures from the crown of thorns,
nails driven into his hands and feet.

Shouldn't Mary's serene face show the pain
a mother would express at the torture and death of her son.
Wouldn't it be easier for every person

to identify with His mother's pain.
This battered and beaten man agonized for our sins.

The mother's loss was eloquently expressed by
    Michelangelo's *Pieta'.*
She cradled His lifeless body in her arms,
finally accepting His fate

Kilnamartyra

I will arise, and go now to Kilnamartyra,
to the rocky, hilly town lands
that birthed my Gaelic ancestors.
I will tread those paths to dream of ancient times.

I will search for their descendants
and ask them to share the legends
told by elders who kept our history.

There will be folk tales of Vikings
who tried to tame the Irish spirit,
warriors who valiantly protected the tribes,
and poets who romanticized them.

In the company of these simple folk
I will find my Celtic soul
and at last I'll know who I am.

Government Issue

What were these golden boys like at 18?
Sports stars wearing letter jackets proudly showing their colors
6A State Champs, Panthers, Cougars, Wildcats. No tattoos, yet.
Girls hanging on their arms
Full of piss and vinegar.

They talked about the foreign lands where they were going.
Talky, Talky, Talky. Nervous. Nervous. Nervous.
Maybe their talk assuaged the fear as they went off to war.
Somewhere deep inside they had to know not everyone
    comes home.
And sometimes it is better if they don't.

After all these years they come to the VA to be mended.
They sit in the waiting room, worn out warriors of years past.
Screaming Eagles, The Chosen Few, Khe Sanh,
Operation Enduring Freedom, Bagram AFB.
History emblazoned on the caps, jackets and tee shirts
    they wear,
arms covered with combat tattoos.
Wrinkled faces, backs hunched over as if dodging bullets.
Some are amputees, others have canes and walkers.
A handful come with spouses who have shared part of the
    warrior's journey.
Others just stare at the 6x6 green floor tiles.
A few of the warriors are still talkers. Are they afraid of the
    silence?
Yet others want to be alone.
Don't bother me with your bullshit.

The conflict might not have killed them,
but they sure as hell were injured.
Their souls will never be the same.

The Gun Range

Thursday afternoon, the parking lot is packed.
What draws this crowd?
A sense of anxiety and curiosity overtake me as I walk up
    the stairs.
Do I really want to go into unfamiliar territory.
Hell yes. I'm 78.
I can go wherever I want.

The sliding door opens and welcomes me inside.
Holy crap. Guns everywhere.
 Assault rifles, machine guns, shotguns, handguns!
And a cafe!
"Please wait to be seated" the sign says.

A man wearing a tight black tee shirt asks, "Can we help
    you sir"?
No thanks, I'm just looking.
And thankfully I am left alone as my eyes like my thoughts
    wander.
I see a table stocked with handguns.
All sizes. Like friggin' cannons they won't fit in my hand.
Go ahead. Make my day.
Others would fit in my pocket.
Ruger, Glock, Smith & Wesson
$495, $650, Used.
I wonder what they were used for.
Did the previous owner's upgrade, or did he just say,

"What the hell am I doing with a gun!!!
I pick up one or two and feel the heft of them.
They bring back memories of a time I owned a handgun
and the sense of power I felt as it nestled in my hand.

Don't anybody mess with me.
Today it just feels like a piece of steel. No power.
I hope the salesperson leaves me alone.
I don't want to answer questions about why I'm here.
"What kind of gun do you want." "What caliber."
"Have you owned guns in the past."
"What do you need a gun for."

I don't need a gun

Unfinished Business

Many came to this nation to escape the poverty and
 oppression that ruled the European continent.
"Give me your tired, your poor, your huddled masses
 yearning to breathe free."
These immigrants supplied the labor to make our nation
 great.
They built cities, roads and schools. There was hope in this
 new land.
There seemed to be opportunity everywhere.
Yet their children had to fight in a "war to end all wars."

Then came the Great Depression in a nation that had the
 most abundant resources in the world.
Still they could not find an answer to harvesting the power
 that lay beneath their feet.
The nation had almost collapsed. And in that collapse. came
 the strength that would make the nation a
beacon of freedom and hope.
Then came World War.

When it was over they marched down Broadway, flags
 waving in the wind,
ticker tape flying from the windows.
The Axis powers had been defeated.
The Greatest Generation had saved democracy for the world.
They went away as kids and came home battle weary and
 hardened.
They gave their hearts and lives to save the world from
 tyranny. When they returned home,
the dream and hope were still there.
But not for everyone.

The long festering sore that lay hidden was ready to tear at the heart of America.
Racism broke open like a pus filled boil.
There was no freedom for the many who saw "Whites only" signs in the their home towns.
The mind of America had to understand what "liberty and justice for all" really means.
Getting their hearts to live those words is the struggle that followed America into the 21st century.

Dreams Abandoned

*"And in that time when men decide
and feel safe to call the war insane,
take one moment to embrace
those gentle heroes you left behind."*

Major Michael O'Donnell,
1 January 1970, Dak To, Vietnam

I stood there in the pouring rain,
wrapped in grief.
I touched his name on The Wall, Panel 28E, Row 48.
James Edward Dooley.

Memories flooded back.
It was the summer of 1955 at Camp Sunrise.
Jimmy was 13, a rambunctious Boy Scout.
Everyone called him carrot top.
He was a hacker, goof off, fun loving,
full of life kid.
He loved to push the limits of convention
and brought great energy to those around him.
From reveille to taps, I always enjoyed being with him.
Then summer was over, Jimmy went home.

Life moved on for me: Military service, college graduation,
marriage, a daughter. Then Vietnam.
Many young men burned draft cards, protested in the
    streets, "Hell no I won't go."

Then I heard Jimmy might have been a casualty.
I didn't know for sure until Labor Day 1992.
And there he was along with 58,177 men and women.

I knew him for only a week, but the grief I felt that day
    when I saw his name on The Wall was for all the
    Jimmys and Janes who did not come home.
A family portrait at the base of one panel said,
"Just wanted you to know we turned out ok. Thank you"
I felt honored to be in their presence.

Slowly I began to see the futility of war.

Wartime Romance

An Irish Roman Catholic Jesuit
and a Flemish underground Jewess:
Charlie could speak English with a Yankee accent and recite
    the Latin mass.
Angelina was fluent in English, French and German.

Their paths crossed in a prisoner of war camp
where he was an army chaplain who ministered to the
    defeated Germans.
And she was assigned to be his interpreter.
Day by day they performed their assigned roles.
The ministry to those who brought terror to others
began to change the way Father Charles looked at his world.

He knew the commitment he made to his church.
would not allow a woman's love to enter his life.
Angelina's daily presence and listening skills
began to nibble away at that commitment.
And an inner struggle for more than words became
    overwhelming at times.

They knew what the ground rules were
in that hellish camp that housed broken men.
Yet they could not quell the love and urgings
that awakened in them.
"Just maybe," they began to hope.

A much needed leave took them to the Swiss Alps,
where skiing gave them freedom to just be.
They sat around a fireplace and talked about the future.
Angelina's homeland lay in devastation and her future
    was uncertain?
His life been promised to God many years ago.

Sadly it could not include this woman he had come to love.
His heart ached because of what could not be.
"Permettez-moi de prendre votre photo Charlie!"
With the Jungfrau and Eiger peaks in the background,
Angelina captured the young Jesuit's smile.
It hid the sorrow in his heart.

Journey Home

From the hill he looked across the dark clay colored valley
and saw the city that appeared in his dreams throughout
    the years
Always a female presence walked with him
Curiously something continually drew him to this place
Here he sought...what?

The original city was made of mud huts,
stacked one against the other
like hovels run down
and crushed together
with only openings in the walls for doors

Over time the city changed shape
and become more modern
Streets ran between the buildings
but there were still no doors, only openings
They beckoned him inside

In all the dreams he was seeking something
He would go from door to door
stopping to look inside
until he found a room to enter.

Some rooms were actually department stores
stocked with numerous gifts
none of which he was looking for.
There the dream always ended
and he left the store unfinished

There was always a female presence
walking with him

so he never felt alone
or fearful in these dream journeys.

The most recent dream changed dramatically
it was in bright technicolor.
He was in a large metropolitan city in a flood
Firetrucks everywhere
His job was to hose them off
and remove the mud.
Among the firefighters a smiling female firefighter
guided him through this task
She had bright red lips that kept moving without a sound

Eventually he walked up the hill and out of the flood waters
When he approached the top he found a crossroad bathed in
    bright light
Looking in all directions he knew he could find his way home
then for the first time his dream brought joy to his heart
because he was no longer lost

Made in the USA
Columbia, SC
21 January 2019